GOD'S

FAVORITE

CREATION

To: Shirley Womack
Alice Brown Hyman

Written by Alice Brown Hyman
Illustrated by Joan D. McNey

Published by:

The McDougal Publishing Company

P. O. Box 3595
Hagerstown, MD 21742-3595

ISBN 1-884369-18-9

Printed in Singapore, for worldwide distribution.

Dedication

To GOD for giving me the vision for this book.

To my grandson, Kyle, the little rainbow which GOD has put in my life.

To the members of my family who supported and encouraged me in this endeavor.

To the late Rev. Joseph A. Miles, founder of the Brookland Union Baptist Church, Washington, D.C., and my pastor for over thirty years. Rev. Miles was a great inspiration to me. He encouraged all of my efforts to serve GOD through my writings and poetry, and gave me many opportunities to do so.

Acknowledgements

Special thanks to:

Ron L. Chase for his artistic expertise and technical advice.

Emily Newman for her encouragement and support.

Jeanne Long for her editorial assistance.

Pastors Charles and Dotty Schmitt of my church — Immanuel's of Silver Spring, Maryland, for their prayers, encouragement, and very helpful suggestions.

All of my many relatives and friends who strengthened me with their prayers, blessed me with their love, and encouraged me with their hope.

The Pastor and congregation of the St. Paul A.M.E. Church of West Newton, Pa., a little town outside of Pittsburgh, whose church was used as the "model" church for the illustrations in this book. I attended many beautiful services at this church as a child growing up in nearby Charleroi, Pa., and as an adult on visits back home.

Dear Parents,

Have you ever felt overwhelmed by your child-rearing responsibilities? Do you feel that you are often inadequate in relating to your children how extremely important and special they are to GOD, and how they are to love and honor HIM?

This book will help children to understand this, and to realize the importance of people to GOD over everything else HE created. It will show them that people — especially children — are HIS favorite creation. HE said in HIS Word, *"Except ye become as little children, ye shall not enter into the kingdom of heaven"* (Matthew 18:3, KJV).

Scripture tells us that GOD formed each of us in our mother's womb (Psalms 139:13) and made us in HIS image to praise and worship HIM. HE created a beautiful world for us to live in, and gave us *"dominion over the fish of the sea, and over the fowl of the air, and over every living thing that moveth upon the earth"* (Genesis 1:28, KJV).

GOD told us to *be fruitful* and to *multiply*. HE has given us the responsibility of nurturing our children by providing spiritual guidance to them, as well as meeting their physical needs. This is truly an enormous responsibility, however, a most rewarding one. As we care for the physical well-being of our children and teach and train them in the ways of GOD, we will have the blessed opportunity of building the foundation for their growth in our love and, most importantly, in GOD's love. We will be able to watch them develop into beautiful children of GOD, real world-changers for HIM, with praise in their hearts and on their lips, which is as HE intended.

Alice Brown Hyman

The **Flower** said, "GOD loves me best. Of all the things HE created, HE has made me more beautiful than the rest!"

The **Tree** said, "Can't you see? GOD's favorite has to be me! HE has made me so big and tall; my limbs reach up almost to the sky. If I am not HIS favorite, just tell me why!"

The **Earth** said, "Pardon me, but I think you both are wrong. I am so pretty all year long. GOD keeps me so green and lovely in summer for all to see."

"In the winter, my mantle is so beautiful and white. Just to behold me is a real delight!"

The **Sun** shouted out and said, "I could not help overhearing the problem among you three. I'm sorry to have to tell you that HIS favorite is me! HE makes me shine so bright and fair; I have to be the one HE holds most dear!"

The **Moon** chimed in, "Just a minute, **Sun**, you are making a great mistake! You just shine when everyone is awake, while I light up the night! I am so bright for all to see, it seems easy to understand GOD's favorite has to be me!"

The **Star** yelled out loud and clear, "I did not want to come right out and say, that I know I am HIS favorite. You may get jealous, you may. But, you remember me, I am the one HE chose to lead the Shepherds and Wise Men long ago. I am a very important star I want you to know!"

"All of you are just wasting time," said the **Brook**, "talking about being GOD's favorite, that I can see. Why, most of you could not get along without me! Water is the most important for people and things, you see!"

"You, **Flower**, **Earth** and **Tree**, you know you could not live without me!"

"You, **Sun**, **Moon** and **Star** may shine ever so bright in the day and in the night. But where would all the creatures you shine upon be if it were not for me? So, I think you have to admit, as far as being GOD's favorite, I just have to be it!"

"Wait a minute," said the **Tree**, "here come some people, let us see what their answer will be!"

"People, can you help us? The problem, you see, is that we are all trying to show how GOD's favorite we each have to be."

"You know us all: **Flower, Earth, Sun, Moon, Star, Water** and **Tree**. Now the question is, who do you think GOD's favorite must be?"

"Well, we don't mean to hurt your feelings," said they. "You are all very important, that we can see. But when it comes to GOD's favorite, of course, it is the people HE created! It just has to be!"

"God created us in HIS own image to praise and worship HIM. HE gave us the power to think, feel and show love to one another in many ways. And, HE made us master of all life upon the earth, in the sky, and in the sea, while HE made each of you to help us and to brighten up our days!"

"**Flower**, you are to beautify our land, planted by GOD's own loving hand."

"And **Tree,** you are to give us shade. That is the reason you were made."

"**Earth**, you provide us with food to eat, like potatoes and tomatoes, pumpkins, melons, carrots and wheat."

"**Sun**, you make it grow. This, we thought surely you would know!"

"**Moon** and **Star**, you light our way as we go along day by day."

"And you, **Water**, quench our thirst, and help to replenish the earth."

"Yes, each one of you is very important, that we all agree. But, we think it should be very easy for all of you to see, that GOD's favorite creation, of course, is the people HE created, and that is the way it is supposed to be!"

I am GOD's FAVORITE CREATION!